Cocaine Addiction Treatment: Hypnotherapy With A 12 Step Treatment Program

Cocaine Addiction Treatment: Hypnotherapy With A 12 Step Treatment Program

H. M. Ford, MA, LPC, NCC, CHt.

To order additional copies of this book, contact:
Xlibris Corporation
1-888-795-4274
www.Xlibris.com
Orders@Xlibris.com
67427

Contents

This book is dedicated to my two older brothers:

Charles, March 6, 1942 to August 7, 1998

and

George, July 30, 1950 to December 21, 2006

Acknowledgements

I have often heard the cliché "no man is an island". The first time I heard it, I thought I understood it well. However, I did not experience the broad context of that statement until I began working on this project.

I would like to acknowledge the following people:

Jillian R. LaVelle, CHt., President of the International Association of Counselors and Therapists for her genuine interest in and encouragement of this project.

Dr. Wil Horton was very instrumental in providing insight into possible reasons for the lack of prior research of this subject.

Anne H. Spencer, CHt., Ph.D., founder of the International Medical and Dental Hypnotherapy Association (IMDHA), Infinity Institute International, Inc. and my former hypnotherapy instructor.

Jerome Beacham, CHt., IMDHA Certification Chairman. He provided me with some priceless information which I thank him for.

Ryan Elliott, MSW, BCD, author of *Wide Awake, Clear-Headed & Refreshed Medical Hypnoanalysis in Action* graciously gave me some clarification.

Gerald Wehmer, CHt., Ph.D., Professor, University of Detroit Mercy. I am exceedingly grateful to him for extending his expertise, guidance and patience with this project.

Most of all, I would like to acknowledge my husband, Kenneth and my son Benjamin. Their sacrifice and understanding while this project was in the making has been great, which makes me appreciate them more than ever.

Author's Notes

When I finished high school and decided to go to college, the most important question I had to ask myself was not whether or not to attend, but what should I study. I have always been genuinely interested in people and wanted to better understand why we do what we do. Therefore, I chose to study psychology in undergraduate school. My professors did an excellent job of giving their students exposure to a full spectrum of psychological theories and applications. Introduction to hypnotherapy was part of that spectrum. I later obtained a separate certification in hypnotherapy.

When I finished my undergraduate studies, I decided to specialize in counseling and enrolled in a Masters degree program in counseling. In order to complete the program, I was required to do a Masters thesis. I was very fortunate to have a research professor who was also certified in hypnotherapy that could supervise a thesis study that involved clinical hypnotherapy applications. The thesis was entitled *Hypnotherapy as an Effective Adjunct Treatment for Cocaine Addiction when used in Conjunction with a 12 Step Drug Treatment Program.* © 2000. This book is an extension of that study.

Chapter I

INTRODUCTION

Does hypnotherapy have positive therapeutic effect on cocaine addicted persons when used in conjunction with a 12 Step Drug Treatment Program? Very little research has been done in this area. However, looking at the events that led up to the modern day version of hypnotherapy, the feasibility of an affirmative result is good.

Early Hypnosis

The early introduction and acceptance of hypnosis was, at best, questionable. The roots of hypnosis started with Franz Mesmer (1734-1815) who was a German physician. He was the pioneer of a practice that became known as "mesmerism". Mesmer had a hypothesis on what caused disease in humans. He believed that physical magnetic fluid existed within the body. This magnetic fluid interconnected every element of the universe. Mesmer believed that disease resulted from disequilibrium of this fluid within the Body. According to Mesmer, the only way to cure the disease was to redirect the fluid through the intervention of a physician. The physician's role was to serve as a type of conduit by which animal magnetism could be channeled out of the universe at large and into the patient's body. This, according to Mesmer, is brought about via "magnetic passes" of the physician's hands.

This theory and process Mesmer introduced brought great controversy among medical practitioners. About 1785, a publication of the *Rapport des Commissaries charges par le Roy de l'examen du magnetisme animal* (Bailly, 1784) concluded that the evidence in favor of mesmeric fluid was inadequate. Mesmer left Paris under a cloud and lived the rest of his life in recluse.

One of Mesmer's disciples was Armand-Marie-Jacques de Chastnet, Marquis de Puysegur (1751-1825). Chastnet was a wealthy aristocrat and landowner who had begun, even before Mesmer's fall, to experiment with magnetic healing. Chastnet is credited with being the founder of modern psychotherapy. While working with Victor Race, a young peasant, the Marquis discovered the "perfect crisis", which was a somnambulistic sleep state. In this state, patients carried out the commands of the magnetizer. Upon reawakening, the patients exhibited no memory for having done so. When Victor, who would never have normally dared to confide his personal problems to the lord of the manor (it would have been an inappropriate disclosure due to class difference), admitted in magnetic sleep that he was disturbed by an argument he had with his sister, Chastnet suggested that he act to resolve the quarrel. Upon reawakening, without memory of Chastnet's words, Victor acted on the Marquis's suggestion. This gave credence to mesmerism and was considered the point of origin of modern psychotherapy.

Since that time, mesmerism has changed names and methods several times and has evolved into present day hypnosis. It is now chiefly used as hypnotherapy. Hypnotherapy has been proven effective in helping some people with weight management, stress reduction, smoking cessation, phobias, pain control, study habits, self-esteem, motivation, sleep deprivation, improving athletic performance, as well as other things.

Definition of Terms

To promote consistency in understanding, definition of a few terms is necessary.

"Hypnosis" is defined in Dorland's Illustrated Medical Dictionary as "a state of altered consciousness, usually artificially induced, characterized by focusing of attention, heightened responsiveness to suggestions and commands, suspension of disbelief with lowering of critical judgment, the potential of alteration in perceptions, motor control, or memory in response to suggestions, and the subjective experience of responding involuntarily."

Dorland's defines "hypnotherapy" as "the use of hypnosis in the treatment of disease."

The same source defines "addiction" as "the state of being given up to some habit, especially strong dependence on a drug."

It further describes "drug addiction" as "a state of heavy dependence on a drug, defined by some authorities as a state of physical dependence characterized by tolerance or withdrawal and by other in a wider sense that includes also emotional dependence, i.e., compulsive or pathological drug use, also referred to as abuse or habituation". The symptoms include tolerance (a need to increase the dose to achieve the desired effect), using the drug to relieve withdrawal symptoms, unsuccessful efforts or a persistent unfulfilled desire to cut down on the drug or stop using it, and continued use of the drug despite knowing of its harm to yourself or others.

The 12 Step Treatment Program

The "12 Step Treatment Program" most often used for drug abuse (other than alcohol) is Narcotics Anonymous (N.A.). "N.A. is a nonprofit Fellowship or society of men and women for whom drugs had become a major problem. We are recovering addicts who meet regularly to help each other stay clean. This is a program of complete abstinence from all drugs. There is only one requirement for membership, the desire to stop using." *Narcotics Anonymous*, Fifth Edition, 1988.

The 12 Steps are:

Step One:	"We admitted that we are powerless over our addiction, that our lives had become unmanageable."
Step Two:	"We came to believe that a Power greater than ourselves could restore us to sanity."
Step Three:	"We made a decision to turn our will and our lives over to the care of God as we understood Him."
Step Four:	"We made a searching and fearless moral inventory of ourselves."
Step Five:	"We admitted to God, to ourselves, and to another human being the exact nature of our wrongs."
Step Six:	"We were entirely ready to have God remove all of these defects of character."
Step Seven	"We humbly asked Him to remove our shortcomings."
Step Eight	"We made a list of all persons we had harmed, and became willing to make amends to them all."
Step Nine	"We made direct amends to such people wherever possible, except when to do so would injure them or others."
Step Ten	"We continued to take personal inventory and when we were wrong promptly admitted it."
Step Eleven	"We sought through prayer and meditation to improve our conscious contact with God as we understood Him, praying only for knowledge of His will for us and the power to carry that out."
Step Twelve	"Having had a spiritual awakening as a result of these steps, we tried to carry this message to addicts, and to practice these principles in all our affairs."

Narcotics Anonymous, Fifth Edition, 1988.

On an outpatient basis, the 12 Step Treatment Program is implemented by the addict attending N.A. meetings (which are held in numerous locations in most communities at various times and days). The addict studies each step and determines how that step applies to him/her. There are speakers (former drug users) at the meetings who share their "story" with the attendees. The attendees share their concerns with each other at the tables where they sit. They give each other input, encouragement and support.

On an inpatient basis, the 12 Step Treatment Program is taught while the addict resides in a treatment facility. There the addict is placed in a group with other addicts, receives individual therapy as well as group therapy, attends classes that educate on how drugs affect the body, mind, the individuals themselves and their families. They are taught coping skills to use when they are faced with situations that would usually trigger them to use drugs. They also attend N.A. meetings during treatment.

The addict, whether inpatient or outpatient status, is encouraged to find a sponsor. A sponsor is someone the addict can establish a positive rapport with. He/she should be someone who was a drug user that has remained abstinent for several years. A sponsor is someone who is willing to be available to the addict when the addict needs to talk because they feel the urge to use drugs and they don't want to give in to that urge. The sponsor is also someone the addict can do positive things with. When an addict is determined to remain drug free and has a good sponsor who is willing to do positive things with them, it helps facilitate a positive lifestyle change.

The 12 Step Treatment Program also stresses that a lifestyle change is necessary for long term abstinence from drug use. Lifestyle changes include but are not limited to the following:

1. Not associating with friends who use drugs
2. Staying away from places where drugs are sold
3. Attending functions that are drug free
4. Making new friends who do not use drugs
5. Setting realistic short and long term goals
6. Learning to face responsibilities
7. Learning to be patient.

Chapter II

LITERATURE REVIEW

Due to the dramatic rise of cocaine use, abuse and dependence, many physical and mental health care professionals have worked with users attempting to discover the best way to help them overcome their addiction.

Cocaine abuse has risen to epidemic proportions in the Western countries. It began in the 1980s when crack (a smokeable, affordable form of cocaine) was introduced. Crack provides an extremely rapid euphoria or "high". Cocaine is one of the most powerful and reinforcing of the central nervous system euphoriant stimulants. Cocaine differs from other drugs of abuse (i.e., alcohol, heroin) in that is commonly used episodically in heavy binges rather than daily. Only a portion of stimulant users (approximately 25%) become compulsive users. Due to the potency of the drug, high rate of addiction and lack of effective treatment methods, cocaine has been termed the most serious psychiatric problem in the United States. (Withers, 1995)

There are several ways to administer use of cocaine. Sniffing cocaine is likely to be the most usual route for social elites. Injecting cocaine and/ or free-basing is more common among polydrug (mainly opiate) users. Crack smoking and has become popular among young, economically deprived people. As cocaine hydrochloride is unsuitable for smoking (it decomposes at high temperatures), users perfected a process which involves freeing the alkaloid from its hydrochloric base using ether.

This process is known as 'free-base'. Another form of cocaine free-base is 'crack'. This is processed by simply cooking the cocaine with baking powder and water. The baking powder draws out the impurities leaving pure, crystalline cocaine. When comparing the different cocaine preparations (free-base method against crack) the difference in the two highs is unmistakable (a peak plasma level of 150 ng/ml compared with a peak plasma level of 800 ng/ml respectively). The majority of people who abuse drugs are aged 20-35 years old. The men to women ratio is approximately 2-3:1(4) + but crack is the most commonly abused drug by pregnant women. (Schifano, 1996).

To date no cure has been found for cocaine addiction and effective treatment of cocaine addiction has not been concrete. There is some promise in contingency management, a form of behavior therapy using community resources such as vocational, educational, financial, and legal counseling together with direct financial rewards for abstinence. This approach has been found to be more effective than the 12 Step program in initiating abstinence and preventing relapse. Pharmacological treatment has not been shown to be effective in itself, but medications that antagonize cocaine by blocking euphoria reduce craving and thus can be valuable when used with non-pharmacological interventions. (Flynn, 1998). One medication, flupenthixol decanote is, in Dr. Platt's words, "possibly the first pharmacological treatment to have demonstrated effectiveness in the treatment of cocaine abuse" (Platt, 1997). Flupenthixol is a xanthene that can be administered intramuscularly at 2-4 week intervals. (Platt, 1997).

Numerous inpatient and outpatient studies have been done to determine if one method of cocaine treatment is more effective than another. One study in particular looked at the effectiveness of the 12-Step program using a combination of disease and enlightenment models versus a relapse-prevention program, using behavioral compensatory strategies.

The result of the study found that both groups had significant post-treatment improvement in relapse prevention skills as measured by the Psycho/Social Information (PSI), but neither group showed greater improvement. Both groups had significantly reduced their use of cocaine at post-treatment follow-up with no difference between groups. (Wells, 1994).

In treatment of cocaine addiction, there is something missing that no one has been able to put their finger on thus far. Reissman suggests that there are two kinds of addictions, simple and complex. They are different in nature and require different approaches to overcome them.

Simple addiction is superficial dependence. It does involve physical craving and withdrawal symptoms when the substance is removed.

However, it is reversible by means of willpower and individual effort. If willpower alone does not alleviate the problem, often meditation and religious practice, exercise, use of herbs, anti-stress techniques, hypnosis, acupuncture and acupressure or other alternative medicines are helpful for tension control and relief from physical dependencies.

However, some people cannot overcome their addiction no matter how hard they try. Those who have a complex addiction experience a psychological hold on them that is far more powerful than their physical need. In these cases, willpower or simple habit-breaking techniques don't work. Complex addiction requires long-term, intensive intervention such as N.A., other 12 Step programs or professional recovery centers and therapeutic communities. When scholars attempt to define addiction, they usually describe the complex form. The key to treatment under this suggestion is proper initial diagnosis so that suitable intervention can be implemented. (Reissman, 1996).

Hypnosis became popular in 1778, when Franz Mesmer first appeared in Paris. Mesmer had a questionable reputation as a miracle worker and there was controversy over the techniques of his treatment which never quite abated. No one was sure how the process worked. However, the practice of magnetizing (which is the first name used for hypnosis) continued. Patients responded and those who practiced it flourished. (Gauld, 1995)

Before techniques of hypnotic induction could come to serve as a tool for research on functional nervous disorders, they had to first be rescued from the domain of pseudoscience to which they had been consigned. Credit for this rescue is generally given to Charles Richet a French psychologist whose "Du somnambulisme provoque" (1875) led to a revival of interest in the scientific use of hypnosis, especially through the work of Jean-Martin Charcot (1825-1893). Charcot began to employ hypnosis in the study of hysteria and discovered that, under hypnosis, he could reproduce not only hysterical symptomatology (amnesia, mutism, anesthesia) but even post-traumatic phenomena. In 1882, Bernheim conceptualized hypnotic phenomena as manifestations of ideomotor suggestibility, a universal human ability to transform an idea directly into an act. For Bernheim, hypnosis was simply a state of heightened, prolonged, and artificially induced suggestibility.

Pierre Janet (1859-1947) studied clinical research under Charcot. Janet developed his own clinical work which included a variety of abnormal mental states which related to hysteria and psychosis. He divided such states into total (involving the whole personality) and partial (part of the personality split from awareness and following its own psychological existence) automatisms. Janet employed automatic writing and hypnosis to identify the traumatic origins and explore the nature of automatism. He also studied multiple personalities, which Janet called "successive existences". It was a short leap from the work of Charcot, Bernheim and Janet to that of Josef Breuer (1842-1925) and Sigmund Freud (1856-1939). (Serendip. 1998)

At present, The American Medical Association and other medical associations have formally recognized hypnosis as a viable medical treatment (Nash, 1999). Hypnotherapy is used not just in the United States but in many countries abroad as well. For example, some people in Great Britain utilize a variety of complimentary medicines to supplement medical treatment. A recent survey revealed that of the top six complimentary medicine methods, hypnotherapy ranked number six (6) of the favorites used. (Goldbeck-Wood, et.al., 1996).

One of the more recent success stories of modern hypnosis is its application in pain control. Hypnosis has been successfully used in management and amelioration of chronic organic pain and for the control of pain and discomfort resulting from certain medical and surgical interventions, childbirth and dentistry. (Hilgard, 1994) It has been clinically proven that hypnotherapy can help cancer patients reduce pain and chemotherapy-related nausea and vomiting (Pattison, 1997). Hypnotherapy can also relieve asthma symptoms and phobias (Harvard Health Letter, 1997).

Clinical hypnosis is a procedure in which a therapist suggests that a client experience changes in sensation, perception, thought and/or behavior. Hypnosis used for clinical purposes is now called hypnotherapy. Hypnotherapy generally includes the addition of hypnosis to some recognized form of psychotherapy (Rhue et al., 1993). As a result, the question to be asked is not whether hypnosis works better than another treatment but rather whether it enhances the effectiveness of a treatment. (Kirsh, 1995).

Before 1980, research on the efficacy of hypnotherapy was largely confined to psychodynamic hypnotherapy (Smith et al., 1980). More recently, empirical studies have focused on the use of hypnosis in behavior therapy, cognitive therapy, and cognitive-behavior therapy (Spinhoven, 1987). Research results reveal that hypnosis can be a useful adjunct to cognitive behavior therapy for a wide variety of problems. (Kirsh, 1995).

Hypnosis has had some success as a treatment modality for drug addiction. An example of this includes an individual case study done with a 24 year old single male who was addicted to cocaine and alcohol. The therapist used a combination of hypnotherapy and related psychotherapeutic treatments as well as requiring the subject to attend

Alcoholics Anonymous (A.A.) and N.A. meetings and do 12 Step program work. The subject was therefore able to maintain complete abstinence. (Orman, 1991).

Another individual case study was done with a 29 year old woman who was addicted to cocaine. She listened to a hypnosis tape for self-hypnosis four times per day which resulted in breaking her cocaine addiction in a period of four months. This study was significant in that hypnosis was the only mode of treatment utilized in this case. (Page, 1992).

Statement of the Problem

The central problem in treating cocaine addicts is that there is no definite therapeutic process that will cure cocaine addiction in the majority of cases. More research needs to be conducted in order to find concrete, scientific methods that can be repeated successfully to provide reliable relief from cocaine addiction. That was the purpose of this study.

Hypothesis

Hypnotherapy has been used to successfully treat other disorders and addictions. It is possible that hypnotherapy, when used in conjunction with a 12 Step drug treatment program, can provide effective relief from cocaine addiction.

Chapter III

METHOD

Participants

This research was conducted by utilizing the case study format. The subjects were selected from an inpatient 12 Step Drug Treatment program located in Michigan in the United States of America.

There were a total of thirty-five (35) respondents to the study's announcement for participants. However, only thirteen (13) of the 35 respondents identified their drug of choice as being cocaine. The other respondents were addicted to either heroin, alcohol or marijuana. The thirteen respondents selected to receive hypnotherapy in this study were all male between the ages of 19-37 years old and were residents in an inpatient 12 Step Drug Treatment program. These participants were placed in Group 2. This group was compared to 13 other male cocaine addicts ages 22-52 years old who also had been inpatient residents in the same 12 Step Drug Treatment program but they did not receive a hypnotherapy session. These participants are in Group 1. The purpose was to determine if there was a difference in the relapse rate between the two groups.

Details of demographic data for each participant are listed in Table 1.

Procedure

It is very important to the safety and well being of the participants that this type of study be conducted by an experienced, certified hypnotherapist. This author is a certified master hypnotherapist with experience in hypnoanalysis, which also includes the clinical application of hypnotherapy. Therefore, the author is well qualified to conduct the hypnotherapy session for this study.

Due to the importance of maintaining the confidentiality of the participants, the name of the treatment facility and management/administration is being withheld. The author met with the onsite clinical supervisor and reviewed the information that would be used in the hypnotherapy session which utilizes guided imagery. The supervisor was in agreement with the study being conducted at the facility with their residents and with the content of the session as the focus was "Relapse Prevention".

The participants voluntarily participated in the study. Ethnographic interviews were conducted with each participant. The interviews included a detailed review of the questionnaire in Appendix C, as well as the individual's phenomenological accounts of the events surrounding their drug use. The participants provided a phone number where they could be reached in the next 30 days for follow up. The study was conducted on December 17, 1999.

Instruments

Examples of instruments used are included. They are not the actual forms. An example of a hypnotherapy induction is included as Appendix A. *IMPORTANT:* Do not use this induction in an attempt to perform a hypnotherapy session yourself. One value most hypnotherapists share is "Do no harm." Hypnotherapy should only be performed by certified hypnotherapists. Contact the author if you need more information. A sample *Client Response Form* is included as Appendix B as it is important to obtain some feedback from those you work with. A background information questionnaire entitled *Intake Record* is included as Appendix C.

Ethics Review

The ethical standards of the American Psychological Association were reviewed by the author prior to initiating the study. As a further safeguard to insure the confidentiality of the participants, a numerical code was assigned to the participants' names. This procedure was conducted as part of the participants' inpatient treatment and again, their participation was voluntary.

This study is very significant. The results will add knowledge to the field of addiction treatment in its search for a more effective, standardized means of treating cocaine addiction.

Chapter IV

RESULTS

The participants in Group 1 did not receive any hypnotherapy. Their only treatment was the inpatient 12 Step Drug Treatment program. When they were contacted 30 days after discharge from treatment, two out of the 13 participants reported they had relapsed. One participant reported he relapsed three (3) days after discharge from treatment. The other participant reported relapse twenty (20) days after discharge from treatment.

The participants in Group 2 did receive one hypnotherapy session and the inpatient 12 Step Drug Treatment program. When participants in Group 2 were contacted 30 days after discharge from treatment, none of those 13 participants reported having relapsed.

Table 1
Descriptive Statistics
Present Age, Age at First Drug Use, Sex, Race and Present Marital Status

Variable	Group 1	Group 2
Present Age Range	22-52 years	19-37 years
Mean	34.23 years	31.77 years
Age at First Drug Use Range	13-39 years	17-36 years
Mean	21.69 years	23.31 years
Sex	Male	Male
Race		
African American	3	2
Hispanic	0	1
Caucasian	10	9
Other	0	1
Present Marital Status		
Married	1	1
Divorced	0	1
Single	12	11

*Group 1 received inpatient 12 Step Drug Treatment program only. Group 2 received inpatient 12 Step Drug Treatment program and one hypnotherapy session.

Chapter V

DISCUSSION

Discussion

The null hypothesis or untested assumption is the rate of relapse is the same for cocaine addicted persons regardless of whether they receive the 12 Step Drug Treatment program alone or the 12 Step Drug Treatment program with hypnotherapy as an adjunct treatment for their cocaine addiction.

There have been no longitudinal studies published at this point in time that would prove or disprove the null hypothesis. At best, individual case studies have been done almost exclusively on a private therapy basis. Due to the fact that the therapy has been private, no comparisons have been done among private patients, most likely in order to maintain confidentiality of the clients.

A weakness of this particular study is that while participants were inpatients in the treatment facility, urinalysis tests were conducted to verify abstinence from drug use. Once the participants were discharged, urinalysis testing could not be done. Therefore, the relapse rate reports were strictly self-reports from the participants and thus unverifiable by the writer.

Summary

The general relapse rate for cocaine addicted persons is approximately 93% using the 12 Step Drug Treatment program alone. Therefore, an adjunct treatment is needed in order to reduce the relapse rate for this population. Hypnotherapy has been used to successfully treat a number of disorders. Therefore, it is possible that hypnotherapy could make a significant difference in relapse prevention for cocaine addicted people if systematically applied with the 12 Step Drug Treatment program.

Conclusion

The actual results of this study indicate that when hypnotherapy was used as an adjunct treatment to the 12 Step Drug Treatment program for cocaine addicted persons, there was approximately a 15% decrease in the relapse rate for the participants during the first thirty (30) days after treatment.

Recommendation

I recommend that hypnotherapy sessions be used on a weekly basis while cocaine addicted persons are inpatient in a 12 Step Drug Treatment program. Once treatment is completed, a longitudinal study should be conducted to track relapse rates of study participants after thirty (30) days, sixty (60) days, ninety (90) days, six (6) months and one year post treatment. This would give a much clearer picture of how effective hypnotherapy is as an adjunct treatment in reducing relapse rates of cocaine addicted persons.

References

1. Page, R. A., & Handley, G.W. (1993). The use of hypnosis in cocaine addiction. *American Journal of Clinical Hypnosis 36:2*, 120-123.
2. Johnson, M. E., & Hauck, C. (1999). Beliefs and opinions about hypnosis held by the general public: a systematic evaluation: *American Journal of Clinical Hypnosis 42:1*, 10-20.
3. Orman, D.J. (1991). Reframing of an addiction via hypnotherapy: a case presentation. *American Journal of Clinical Hypnosis 33:4*, 263-271.
4. Kirsch, I., Montgomery, G & Sapirstein, G. (1995). Hypnosis as an adjunct to cognitive-behavioral psychotherapy: a meta-analysis. Journal of *Consulting and Clinical Psychology 63* (2), 214-220.
5. Merskey, H. (1996). A history of hypnotism: contemporary international hypnosis. Proceedings of the thirteenth international congress of hypnosis, Melbourne, Australia, 6-12 August, 1994. *Psychological Medicine 26* (6), 1283-1285.
6. Serendip (1996). Trance and trauma: functional nervous disorders and the subconscious mind. Serendip.brynmawr.edu/Mind/ Trance.
7. Larkin, M. (1999). Hypnosis makes headway in the clinic. *The Lancet, v353i9150*, 386 (1).
8. Goldbeck-Wood, S., Dorozynski, A., Lie, L. G., Yamauchi, M., Zinn, C., Josefson, D., & Ingram, M. (1996). Complementary medicine is booming worldwide. *British Medical Journal, v313n7050*, 131 (3).
9. Schifano, F. (1996). Cocaine misuse dependence. *Rapid Science Publishers 9*, (3), 225-230.

10. Heap, M. (1995). Hypnosis in the relief of pain. *The British Journal of Psychiatry, 166* (5), 694.

11. Pattison, J. (1997). Hypnotherapy: complementary support in cancer care. *Nursing Standard, 12* (52), 44-46.

12. President and Fellows of Harvard College (1997). Hypnosis: more than a suggestion. *Harvard Health Letter, v22n12,* 4 (2).

13. Reissman, F., & Carroll, D. (1996). A new view of addiction: simple and complex. *Social Policy, 27,* 36-46.

14. Withers, N. W., MD, Ph.D.; Pulvirenti, L., MD; Koob, G. F., Ph.D.; & Gillin, J. C., MD. (1995). Cocaine abuse and dependence. *Journal of Clinical Psychopharmacology, 15* (1), 63-78.

15. Wells, E. A., Peterson, P. L., Gainey, R. R., Hawkins, J. D., Catalano, R. F., & Frances, R. J., MD. (1995). Outpatient treatment for cocaine abuse: a controlled comparison of relapse prevention and twelve-step approaches. *Year Book of Psychiatry & Applied Mental Health, 5,* 165-166.

16. Flynn, W. R., MD (1998). Cocaine addiction: theory, research, and treatment. *The American Journal of Psychiatry, 155* (8), 1128-1129.

17. Spencer, A.H., Ph.D. (1995). Clinical hypnoanalysis induction techniques. *Infinity Institute International, Inc.,* 1-4.

Appendix A

EXAMPLE INDUCTION FOR HYPNOTHERAPY

Disclaimer:

The following induction is an example only. It is not to be used in a real hypnotherapy session. Hypnotherapy should only be performed by an experienced, certified hypnotherapist.

Appendix A

EXAMPLE INDUCTION FOR HYPNOTHERAPY

Disclaimer:

The following induction is an example only. It is not to be used in a real hypnotherapy session. Hypnotherapy should only be performed by an experienced, certified hypnotherapist.

Beginning of Induction:

Are you ready to begin? (Wait for response). First, get into a comfortable position in your seat with your hands resting one on each leg and your feet flat on the floor. That's it—get comfortable. Look at the ceiling and find a spot that you can focus on. It may be a spot or small crack. Any spot on the ceiling you can focus on will do. Good. Now take a deep breath, deep breath and let it out slowly. Excellent!

Focus your eyes on the spot on the ceiling and concentrate on it. Stay focused on the spot on the ceiling. Keep your eyes on the ceiling. As you continue to watch the spot, it will become a little fuzzy. Watch it. Watch the spot on the ceiling. Concentrate on the spot on the ceiling. As you watch the spot on the ceiling, your eyes will become heavy, become heavy. Your eyes are growing heavier and heavier, heavier and heavier, heavier and heavier, growing heavier and heavier . . . and heavier . . . heavier . . . until they close. (Pause)

I am going to count from three down to the number one. With every number I count, I would like for you to take a deep breath, and each time I say the word "relax", I would like for you to relax and allow the breath to rush from your body. With every number I count, take a deep breath, and each time I say the word "relax", I would like for you to relax and allow the breath to rush from your body.

Three, take a deep breath (pause) and relax. Good. Two, take a deep breath, deep breath, and relax. One, deep breath . . . and relax. Relax your thoughts, relax your body. Good, very good, now continue to breathe normally.

I'm going to count from three down to one again. I would like for you to mentally release each group of muscles that I call to your attention.

Three (pause), release the muscles in your neck and shoulders. Feel your head slowly drop forward.

Two, release the muscles in your back and allow your hands to assume a comfortable position.

One, release the muscles in your stomach and feel the relaxation flow down through your legs and feet.

Like a series of dominoes, all the muscles in your body begin at the top of your head and flow one into another as each one releases and relaxes.

Good. Now I would like for you to use your imagination. Imagine a gentle water wave, like an ocean wave. A wave of warming, soothing relaxation, gently rushing up over your body and rushing back down again, taking with it all the tensions, all the strains and bathing you in a sea of warming, soothing relaxation. It is rushing up over your body and rushing back down again, taking with it all the tensions, all the strains.

A wave, like an ocean wave, rushing up over your body and rushing back down again, bathing you in a sea of warming, soothing relaxation, allowing you to relax, causing you to relax. Relax and go deeper . . . deeper and deeper . . . deeper and deeper. With every beat of your heart, with every breath you take, you will become more relaxed, more sleepy, more drowsy. (Pause for 3 seconds) take a deep breath (pause) and relax. Relax and go deeper. Deeper and deeper.

Excellent! Now I would like for you to imagine a well-lit flight of stairs—ten steps in all—leading up to a large double door. Imagine a well-lit flight of stairs—ten steps in all—leading up to a large double door. I'm going to count to ten and with every number I count, I would like for you to mentally take one step, and by the time I have reached the number ten, the doors will open and you will cross over the threshold, into the most beautiful place you could ever imagine.

One, take the first step.

two, take the second step.

Three . . . four . . . five . . . six . . . seven . . . eight . . . nine . . . ten.

The doors open and you cross over the threshold, into the most beautiful place. The most beautiful place you could ever imagine. (Pause)

As you mentally walk though this most beautiful place, touch the ground. What does it feel like? (Pause) Smell the air. What fragrances do you perceive? (Pause) Is the sky cloudy or clear? (Pause) Are there any living creatures nearby? (Pause)What do you hear? See it . . . smell it . . . touch it. Use all your senses. (Long pause).

Excellent. You are learning to use a highly specialized part of your brain using guided imagery. Through guided imagery, you interact directly with your body. You can open lines of communication between your body and your mind.

Relax your mind, relax your body. Relax . . . relax. Now listen to my voice and only my voice. Listen only to me and allow your thoughts to fill with the positive things I say. All other sounds which you may hear will have only a calming, soothing effect.

As you go deeper and deeper relaxed, deeper and deeper with every breath you take, I'm going to talk to you about the convalescent stage in treating the problem of addiction. Now as you go deeper and deeper and I give you these positive suggestions, they take complete, thorough and immediate effect upon you.

Your drug problem is over. That's been straightened out completely. And furthermore, you know it. You are drug-free and you're completely drug-free. You have no desire for drugs in any way. You don't need them, you don't want them and they are no longer a part of your life. Most of all, you are proud. Proud because you are on top.

You are really on top now. You don't have anything to prove. You have already proved it. You have proven yourself as an adult. You have proved yourself as being mature. You proved that you can positively function in society. You have proven you can earn a living. You have proven that you can study, that you can think, that you can read, that you can go forward and be a complete and fulfilled person. But even more than that, you have proved your ability to conquer the most difficult problem on earth. A drug problem. Which is something that, if other people who were not aware of that problem were faced with it, they might not be able to surmount it at all. Yet you have done it. You have proved yourself even more than most people.

It is very important—now that you have proved yourself, now that you are drug-free and you are on top—to stay there. The maintenance of your sobriety is important. It is just as important as getting drug-free itself.

When a person has had pneumonia or tuberculosis, even though they are completely well, it would not be wise for them to take a job as a sand-hog and expose themselves to elements that would cause the disease to flare up. For this reason it is very important that even though you are completely drug-free, do not allow yourself to go to places where you would be exposed to drugs you once used or were tempted to use. You can avoid a flare up. Stay away from those places to give yourself time to convalesce and stay strong.

As you refrain from going places where drugs are, you become stronger and stronger with every day that passes. Strong in body, strong in mind, strong in spirit. You are going to be very happy and contented because you have licked the problem you had with drug use; not partially, but completely, thoroughly, one-hundred percent. Because you enjoy being on top, you are going to avoid drugs like they are the plague. You are going to avoid places where drugs are like you would avoid the plague.

It is important that you have a certain amount of time to develop complete stability in every area of your life. You want to be stable, adequate and effective. Your drug-free status is permanent in every way and it's going to stay that way. Your freedom from drug use is final and you are safe.

Stable . . . Adequate . . . Final . . . Effective. Those four words are important. Their initials spell SAFE. You are going to remember it and never forget it. Stable, Adequate, Final, Effective—SAFE. You are going to remember it and never forget it. You are going to be SAFE.

"S" stands for Stable. You are going to be stable, more stable than you have ever been in your life.

"A" stands for Adequate. You are going to be adequate, very adequate in every way, all the time.

"F" stands for Final. Your drug-free status is permanent and final in every way. You will not let anything or anyone (including yourself) cause you to use drugs again.

"E" stands for Effective. You are going to be effective in your work, play and in every single area of your life. You are going to do every positive thing you can to continue to be SAFE.

Now relax, relax and let these suggestions take complete and thorough effect upon you mind, body and spirit, sealing itself in the deepest part of your subconscious mind, never to be forgotten.

You are SAFE—Stable, Adequate, Final and Effective. When you have any difficulty or challenges that cause you to think you should return to using drugs, you are going to remember the word S.A.F.E. and the suggestions it stands for. Use it to help you when you have difficulty or challenges. Now relax deeply and be SAFE in every way. (Pause).

Now take a deep breath, exhale, and relax. All the suggestions I have given you are now strongly implanted, are part of you now, and will remain with you for as long as they are positively useful to you. In fact, with every breath you take, with every beat of your heart, the suggestions are growing stronger and are becoming your new habits for health.

Now I am going to count from one to ten, and with every number that I count you will slowly become alert.

One, two, three, four, five, six, seven, eight, nine, ten. You are completely alert, feeling refreshed and relaxed.

Appendix B

CLIENT RESPONSE FORM

Appendix B

CLIENT RESPONSE FORM

Date: _____

Focus: Hypnotherapy Guided Imagery to assist with Relapse Prevention

Client Name: _____

Phone number where you can be reached for follow up in the next 30 days: _____

Drug of Choice: _____

Indicated below is my response to this session:

_____

_____

_____

Would you recommend this session to others? Yes ____ No ____

Why or why not? _____

_____

_____

Appendix C

INTAKE INFORMATION

Intake Information

Personal Information:

Name: _____ Date of Birth: _____ Age: _____

Marital Status: _____ Number of children and their ages: _____

Client's Sex: __ Weight: __ Height: __ Eye Color: __ Hair Color: __ Build: __

Race: African American __ Asian __ Caucasian __ Hispanic __ Other _____

Affect and Appearance: _____

Are you currently thinking of hurting yourself or anyone else?

Are you currently in any physical pain? If so, rate level of pain with 1 being very minimal to 10 being unbearable. Circle answer: 1 2 3 4 5 6 7 8 9 10

What prompted you to come for treatment at this time? _____

_____

Education: Circle answer

High School Diploma   GED Certificate   Associates Degree   Trade School Certificate   Undergraduate Degree   Graduate Degree   Doctorate Degree

Current Employment Status: Circle answer

Employed Full Time   Part Time   Student   Unemployed   Not Looking   Disabled

What is your usual occupation? _____

Veteran Status: Circle answer

Currently on Active Duty   Reservist   Veteran   Disabled Veteran

Mental Health History:

Have you had any previous outpatient mental health treatment? Yes __ No __

If yes, explain: _____

_____

Have you had any psychiatric hospitalizations? Yes __ No __

If yes, explain: _____

_____

Are you now or have you in the past taken any psychiatric medications?
Yes __ No __

If yes, which ones and explain what they were taken for: _____

_____

Physical Health:

Describe your current physical health status? _____

Are you receiving treatment for any medical condition? Yes __ No __

If yes, list condition(s) and medications you are taking: _____

_____

Legal Issues:

Have you ever been arrested: Yes __ No __

If yes, list number of arrests, convictions, what they were for and your
current legal status: _____

_____

Was drug use a factor in your legal issues? Yes __ No __

_____

Expectations from Treatment:

The benefit you obtain from treatment is not dependent upon others. Staff will be supportive in giving you information and suggestions you can use to facilitate abstinence from drug use and relapse prevention. The success of your treatment is a direct result of your application of the things you learn to your life. This requires that you make and keep a commitment to yourself to remain drug free both during and after treatment.

SPECIAL OFFERS:

Order these visual aids to remind you that you are S.A.F.E.:

	Price Each	Number Ordered	Total
12 Month Appointment/Planner 8.5" x 5.5"	$21.95	_____	_____
12 Month Wall Calendar 11" x 12"	$14.95	_____	_____
8 oz. Coffee Mug	$10.50	_____	_____
Imprinted Key Chain	$5.50	_____	_____
Sub Total			_____
Tax			_____
Shipping and Handling			$ 6.95
Grand Total			$ _____

Customer Name: _____

Address: _____

Daytime phone: _____ Email: _____

Payment Method:

Check/Money Order

Master card or Visa Card Number: _____

Expiration Date: _____ 3 Digit Code on back of card: _____

I certify I am the cardholder or authorized user for the above credit card and do authorized H.M. Ford Company to charge this card for the items ordered above.

Print Name: _____ Signature: _____

Mail the completed order form to: H.M. Ford Company, Special Offers, P.O. Box 579, Mount Clemens, MI 48046. Orders are shipped via U.S. Postal Service in 10 to 14 days of order receipt.

NEWSLETTERS

H.M. Ford Company also produces newsletters on various mental health issues. If you would like to be put on this mailing list, fill in your information below and mail to:

H.M. Ford Company, Newsletters, P.O. Box 579, Mount Clemens, MI 48046.

Name: _____

Address: _____

City: _____ State: _____ Zip: _____

Email: _____

Phone: (_____) _____

Topics you are interested in: _____

Occupation: _____